by Francine Cardone Miller

blurred vision

One Woman's Memoir of Looking Beyond Abuse, Alcoholism, and Codependency

TATE PUBLISHING & *Enterprises*

Published by Tate Publishing & Enterprises, LLC
127 E. Trade Center Terrace | Mustang, Oklahoma 73064 USA
1.888.361.9473 | www.tatepublishing.com

Tate Publishing is committed to excellence in the publishing industry. The company reflects the philosophy established by the founders, based on Psalm 68:11,
"The Lord gave the word and great was the company of those who published it."

Published in the United States of America

ISBN: 978-1-60696-545-0
1. Biography & Autobiography: Personal Memoirs
2. Family & Relationships: Abuse: Domestic
09.02.20

blurred vision

Dedications

Dedicated first:

I dedicate this book first to God and then to my husband, John, who honors my journey, believes in me as a beloved daughter of a heavenly Father, and inspires me with his infinite wisdom and insight each and every day.

And second:

To my beloved eight children:

John Robert–the mighty samurai

Antoinette–free spirit

Jake–peaceful warrior

Anna–inspirational at every turn

Isabella–honest, loving, giving

Luke–dragon slayer

Raquel–the joyous dancer

Adam–pure joy

And third:

To all the people in the world who have been affected by the powerful affliction of alcoholism.

Foreword

This diary is dedicated to all of the people in the world who are involved or have ever been involved in a painfully dysfunctional, verbally, physically, or emotionally abusive relationship and/or who struggle with the pain, the loneliness, and the torture of alcoholism. Let us all as a human race empower ourselves to stop the pain of abuse. Let us look into the soul and heart of self and find courage, peace, and true freedom. I am not a therapist; however, this is merely my true story, my diary.

I grew up with an alcoholic father. He died at sixty of cirrhosis of the liver. Regardless of my attempts to recognize the pain and suffering of my parents and to know in my heart that I wanted a different life for myself, I was drawn like a magnet to an alcoholic, and I married him. At first the relationship was good, and it seemed healthy. But as time progressed, as we began to live life, the alcoholism revealed itself more and more. The sickness of the relationship fed an inner feeling in me that I hadn't let go of, that I hadn't worked through. I hadn't healed the pain of my childhood experiences. I hadn't faced the issues of who I was and who I could potentially become. I simply hadn't done the work on myself to be able to embrace and create healthy relationships.

I understand the feelings to stay in an abusive relationship for fear of the unknown, fear of facing self. I understand the denial, the covering up to the world, the constant compromising and selling out of your own inner values and truths. I understand how incredibly difficult it is to leave someone who is hurting you. I understand the inner doubt that on some level you think you deserve it. I understand how great the desire is to change other people, to try to fix their lives, to help them find their true potential, to save the alcoholic. In the meantime, while trying to fix others, our own lives, our own emotional makeup, our own spirits become desperately neglected. I understand the unbearable loneliness and pain that comes from making a great change in your life and standing up for truth. I understand that loss of control sometimes feels like loss of life itself. I understand!

I remember the intense feelings of anger for the alcoholic. I remember how abused, neglected, frustrated, and resentful I was toward him. I realized that even though he drank, abandoned me, and abused me, I on some subconscious level consented to the pain. I stayed, I listened, I participated, and I chose to neglect and abandon myself. Our dialogue became as sick as the sickness itself. Change is difficult. One must pull from the very essence of self, from the core of one's being, from God, to find the courage to change.

If your spirit tells you you're in pain, you are. If spirit tells you something is wrong in your relationship, something is wrong. If spirit is desperately searching or longing for truth, peace, and love, seek after these feelings, for they are there for all of us to discover. It is up to us to have the courage to face the pain and reality of our own life, to diligently turn the power over to a source greater than ourselves, to have the courage to do the work necessary to save our own souls, and to finally experience the peace, freedom, comfort, and joy that comes from the hard work of healing and recovery.

This is an account of my journey; it is private, painful, and revealing to the devastating perils of alcoholism, but it is also full of hope for the grace of God that is within all of us. My prayer is that this diary will be a catalyst for truth, healing, and inspiration for anyone who is struggling to find his or her true potential. We are all children of a fair and merciful God. He loves us and wants us to discover the true potential of our divine natures; there are always roadblocks along the way. I share this diary as a testimony of the pain our spirits suffer when we are enmeshed in a dysfunctional relationship and off the track of discovering ourselves, but more so as a source of healing. We are not alone. Keeping this diary set me free, for one of mankind's greatest struggles is that we forget too easily from whence we came. It is important that we remember for today, look back for a season, and then let go and move forward, for tomorrow is full of hope, joy, freedom, and forgiveness.

September 1, 1991

Dear Diary,

Today is the first day, the cathartic day. I have given myself permission to write in my diary and to free my mind and my heart of the thoughts of my pain. It is my personal endeavor. I fully submerge my will to that which is higher than me, that which I have no control over. Yet I hesitate; I fear. How free am I? How safe can I be? Will my thoughts be read and known by all, or am I granted the privacy and serenity of my own diary? Does God hear me? Does he read my words? I am afraid!

The vomit fills my stomach. My mind is a torture chamber. I am dying. Am I in hell? I have indeed created my own reality, yet the reality of my life fills my bowels with bile. Suddenly I am stopped by my daughter of two. She is running around the car wearing blue, singing, yelling, "Watch this, Momma. I'm dancing like a fairy, la, la, la, la." What joy to see, thank you.

October 28, 1991

How could I mourn over hell when I am in hell slowly dying day by day? I tell myself to keep my solid-ground young flower. Don't allow the perils of one man—his moods, his anger, his temperament, and verbally abusive tone—rattle my petals. He walks into the room like a thunderstorm gone sour, *thump, thump*. I hear his footsteps; my skin begins to crawl. I see the growl and bitter look on his face.

The children are decorating the front porch for Halloween. They are full of excitement and joy. He walks by and growls, "I'm not cleaning this crap up! Don't you think they have overdone it?"

I am aware of the intensity of his energy. I could cut the negative energy in the house with a knife. My mind is overwhelmed. I have an exam tomorrow at college, I am supposed to substitute fifth grade, the baby is crying, the chicken is cooking, and I need help. He is locked in the back room. He stays in there unavailable for the children, for me, for life. I ask him to come to dinner, and he yells, "I know when the !@#$ to come out for dinner." He never comes. We eat alone, we cry alone, we laugh alone, we struggle alone, yet there is a stranger in the house, a sadness that overshadows us all.

I am afraid that if I make him angry he will leave and go to the bar. He will drink, and then he will come home again. Yet he seems to want to be angry regardless of what I say or do. Maybe I am being set up to play into his inner desire to leave anyway. I try to have everything done—the house clean, dinner, the kids fed. Does it really matter what I say or do? I live in fear of his moods and his anger, but he will do what he will do. Maybe tomorrow will be better. My stomach hurts.

Again my sweet daughter interrupts the thick cloud of turmoil with a sweet wave of her hand and a twist of her head. She says, "Momma, I'm Piglet." I love her!

October 29, 1991

The shower is on, a moment for me to breathe in peace. I feel the warmth of the hot water on my shoulders. I think that I shall stay in there forever. Eventually the water turns cold, and I must get out. He will return again soon, and I shall be thrown back into the chambers of hell.

I have the will to be free of torture and ignorance. I have the will to be free from the torment of verbal abuse and cruelty. He does not seem to care or think about his relationships with his world, his family, his children, or even himself. He fears the world, he trusts no one, and he has no self-esteem. Then why would I ever expect him to believe in me?

I have faith. I must have faith. I must have faith. I will greet this day with love in my heart. I will great this day with love in my heart, for love is the greatest foundation toward success. Love me, love me, please, someone love me.

November 23, 1991

As much as I know, I must change my life somehow. He is hurting me daily. The words fall upon my spirit. Part of me feels deaf, and I wonder whom he is talking about. Yet I also feel the words hammering my head; they hammer my consciousness. I am completely drained and depleted. I cannot feel my heart, my mind, or my soul. I have become so desensitized to the abuse that I cannot feel myself. It feels as if his goal is to strip me away of all that I am. Yet how can someone have such power over me? The house tonight is like a war zone. Am I still not free to laugh, to live? Am I doomed only to cry?

He criticizes my clothes. He questions my integrity. He accuses me falsely. He yells and screams at me. If I say the wrong thing, he goes into a bitter rage. He trusts no one. He imposes his fears, his own inadequacies, onto me. He says I am naïve and weak and the world will take advantage of me. He says I have an unrealistic fantasy of people; he says I live in a fairy tale. He gets angry when I cry. He screams that I am a big baby and for me to toughen up. He is hurting me, and I feel too sad to cry. I feel hurt and sad. My insides feel shattered. What am I to do?

November 25, 1991

I am trying to recover from the flu. Today I feel better and better. I am drained though. I tried to rest. I lay awake all weekend alone. He is on a drinking binge. When he comes home—I don't know when—he will be so angry. He is angry with me, at the children, but he seems to hate himself the worst. I lay awake unable to sleep, to study, to cry, to act, or to move. The television has become my mind; I completely surrender to the hypnotic state.

He comes home. He is drunk, angry, and violent. I cannot hide. I am unable to move, yet he will not leave me alone. I am angry at him. Why is it that he goes out and drinks all weekend, abandons his family, hurts his family, and is angry at me? Where is the peace? Where is the justice? I'm worried about the children.

We have two children living with us. My son is six; he is from a previous relationship of mine. We have one daughter together. She is two. He doesn't relate to my son too well. He tries to parent him at times. He admits openly that his father barely spoke to him and when he did, it was demeaning. He isn't sure how to speak or to parent the children. We talked a lot about these issues before we were married. I was petrified of repeating my own painful childhood dynamics. Before we were married, we went to counseling. We worked on parenting issues in therapy, along with alcoholic issues and dysfunctional-relationship issues. Now that he is drinking again, he has stopped using the tools we gained from our counselor.

November 29, 1991

We made cookies tonight. My son brought him a cookie and a glass of milk. He hit the plate away. He said he didn't want that crap. The child was devastated. His act of kindness was destroyed. The boy is seeking guidance. How will he learn to trust? Never again will a child full of love bring a man, whose heart is full of hate, a gift of food. I can not explain the look on this child's face, the disappointment; the rejection; the loss of love, trust, and respect. He was told, "Get the hell out of here!"

It wasn't always like this. His heart is good; he used to be kind and considerate. Before we were married, he was sober three years. He was involved in the family. He was helpful around the house. He worked hard. We set goals as a family. He coached my son's T-ball games. He said he wanted to be the dad that he never had. I trusted him. Somewhere along the way he gave up. He stopped dreaming about a future, he stopped caring about himself, and he stopped working on our family.

December 12, 1991

The pattern of his mood swings continues, yet we have experienced days, weeks, of peace. I am confused. I feel the calmness of the weeks past. I so desire peace. I want good things for my family. I start to hope that maybe things will change.

He is gone drinking again. Here I am again in the lion's den, alone, afraid, angry, tired, waiting for him. I feel completely abandoned. Who can I turn to? Where is the hope? Does it lie in the days of calm? Am I holding on for sheer survival? I cling to those days when I feel peace and calm. I cling to the memories of what used to be. Then suddenly he comes home so angry. He hides away. He won't talk about anything. The rule is don't talk, don't think, don't evaluate, don't question, so we don't have to change. My head is exploding. My spirit senses the intolerance of this situation. My spirit is crying out desperately, and I feel so trapped.

He went through a one-year alcoholic program at the veteran's hospital and recovery house. He knows the devastating effects of alcoholism on the family and on himself. He can die—he almost did. We both know and understand the disease. Therefore, we are both responsible for the choice to stay in this pain and deny the reality of our life. We need help. We cannot continue on this path. I know that something must change. Where can I find the strength? He will not listen, or talk, or evaluate, or change.

December 14, 1991

God must grant me the serenity of something. Without God I am nothing. The stress builds. I snap at the children; I have finals this week. I am so tired. I am too tired to fight, to change, to have courage. We saw Santa alone, we ate dinner alone, we did homework alone, and we read stories alone. I am dead. I am in prison, a prison that I have on some level consented to. I experience great highs at school. I love life, learning, the excitement of discovery, yet how am I managing to keep it all together? How can I love learning and the concept of freethinking, how can I reach my true potential, when my life is in such turmoil?

I feel as if he fooled me. He made me believe, or maybe I wanted to believe, there were hope, love, and peace in family unity. I reflect upon the years we spent in counseling before our marriage. We worked in therapy together. We set goals together and made promises together. We both were able to understand the pain of our childhood experiences and how these experiences played themselves out in our lives together. What has happened? Where did the sickness of alcoholism sneak back into our home? I must face the truth.

January 8, 1992

By the grace of God, I have been able to finish my finals. I have almost completed the teacher-credential program. In the meantime, I have been able to substitute teach on my off days. I feel a great sense of myself when I teach. I feel an incredible connection to the kids. I have one semester left, and I am done with school.

I had a dream about a movie in the future. I dreamt about a woman of substance, an epic goddess, a female hero. The movie was for the children of the nineties. The children of today need a positive, reflective, female role model who demonstrates courage, independence, and self-assurance. I dreamt about the Madonna—mother of Jesus. How did she see life? What were her challenges, her struggles, and her obstacles? Yet she had sweet Joseph to love her, honor her, and support her. Does Joseph exist in the world today? I feel the woman's spirit, the woman warrior who stands up for truth, who fights for freedom of spirit and individuality. Maybe it is I who needs a role model.

January 9, 1992

He will never understand me. We have no intimacy. My heart and mind are longing for understanding, closeness, respect, truth, and cooperation. What is intimacy? What is marriage? What does it all mean? I think back upon my parent's marriage, and I see images of abuse, anger, and my mother broken. I remember her ceramic artwork shattered against the fireplace and wine being thrown into faces. I remember her blackened eyes swollen shut and her tortured spirit. As a child something inside me powerfully sensed the wrongs of those actions, just as now I sense the wrongs of my relationship.

Spirit knows. It knocks for freedom and goodness, yet somehow I have become desensitized and tolerant of the pain and abuse. I inflict it as well as receive it. Why? Should I not look too deeply into the minds of man or woman? I cannot shake this feeling of rejection and aloneness. Over and over again I feel so alone and abandoned. It is not acceptable to speak, to ask, to talk. If I don't question the reality, then I don't have to think, and therefore I don't have to change. Why do I stay?

January 10, 1992

Today his words are like tiny knives, piercing my heart and my soul. I tried to speak of change, intimacy, relationships, family unity, and goals. He tells me to leave things alone, to quit thinking, to quit talking, and to quit arguing. He now lives in a different world than I do. He doesn't desire what I desire. He is simplistic. He wants food, sex, and the bar, and he wants to complain endlessly with no hope in sight. He is verbally abusive one minute and sorry the next. Everything is negative. Nothing works. No one is to be trusted. The world is black or white. He left this morning for the bar.

Freedom is my word for the week. What is freedom? I wish to live free to be able to live my life, to become happy, to experience joy, to be intellectually and spiritually stimulated, to know God, to be alive! Someone help me, please.

January 11, 1992

I feel the black plague that has swept across my life. I feel consumed and overwhelmed by the negative, yet my innate nature desires truth, creativity, love, and positive feelings. Is God testing me? I wonder if I am destined to be forever alone. Is that all I can ultimately experience in life, aloneness? I care for him, yet will I ever get over this pain? I try to believe that I am in a relationship that is workable. I think about our past and the work we did in recovery. Maybe we can compromise, but is there a compromise with alcoholism? Can we escape its claws without facing it head on?

We keep avoiding the issue as if it doesn't exist. He goes days without drinking, and then it hits him hard. He usually binges for a few days of non-stop drinking. He can start at eight in the morning and drink around the clock without food for three or four days. He is killing himself, and I am dying right along with him. He is still not home.

January 12, 1992

It is the morning after. He is asleep in one of the children's beds. He left here two days ago at one in the afternoon and returned after eleven tonight. I feel as though he has no consideration for us as a family. He never calls. I hate him! I don't trust him, and I don't respect his values. I cannot have faith and freedom in my relationship. How can I move beyond the lack of trust? There is too much history. Where can I find forgiveness? Alcoholism lies, it betrays, it abandons, it manipulates. It takes good men from their families and destroys lives.

It was easier before I knew anything about the disease. I know the work that must be done, yet I cannot change him. He hasn't worked in three weeks. The rain has become my enemy. When it rains he doesn't work. He gets depressed, so he spends all afternoon at the bar.

I promised myself today that I would never speak again. Please remove my tongue for it serves no purpose, remove my mind for I am not free to use it, remove my soul for it is encased in a tightly webbed seduction of negativism. Hamlet once said, "to be or not to be," meaning should I live or should I die. I choose to live!

I had a dream of a poor girl on the street. She somehow picks herself up, challenges herself. She does the work, and she becomes a teacher. How sensitive she is to the needs of those around her. How well she knows the suffering of the poor, the hurt, and the abused.

June 2, 1992 (four months later)

He has been sober; at least he has abstained from drinking, for a time. We bought a house together, and suddenly the house took the focus off of the disease and our problems. Did he buy me off, or did I sell out for new dreams, new hopes? Maybe things will change. The children love the pool. The home feels safe to me. He seems committed to taking care of the house, yet he struggles to take care of us. He is still angry all the time. He doesn't go to meetings. He doesn't work a program; he merely abstains from alcohol.

June 23, 1992

Somehow through sheer denial we have made it through to summer vacation. We have moved into our new house. The kids are so excited. Maybe this was his way of saying let's try to make it work. The house feels so nice. I planted fresh flowers out front. The children have new friends and a new school. We are at peace for the day.

He has recognized the pain we are all in and committed to not drink. Is not drinking enough? I remember four years ago when he went through the veteran's alcoholic center. His liver was twice the size. He had pneumonia and was close to death. They told him if he did not stop drinking he would die. After going through that very difficult alcohol program, we attended therapy for three years. All of these memories haunt me because we both have knowledge of the damage and pain alcoholism causes a family. He knows all too well the commitment it takes to be clean and sober. It is a total change of lifestyle.

He was sober for so long. How did it slip back into our reality? On some level we both consented. He never was able to accept that there was a higher power. He thought people were crazy when they talked about turning their lives over to God. He went to a few AA meetings, but he was really critical of the people. He doesn't trust anyone, so he couldn't find someone to sponsor him and to help him.

August 1, 1992

I am reminded today of the work I had to do when we began therapy and of the changes I had to make. In therapy we worked heavily on our childhood experiences, but we also worked on developing ourselves. We worked on each person being a separate individual and developing, loving, and nurturing self. The focus was not on the other person but on taking responsibility for self regardless of how the other person is acting. The focus was being honest with each other and communicating our feelings. The hardest part for me was to know how I felt about anything.

Since he began drinking again, I can see that I am a codependent. I am tied up in his view of the world and of me. When he is healthy, I feel good. When he is angry, I am afraid. When he is happy, I feel relief. For as sick an alcoholic as he is, I am an equally sick codependent. Even now I can see that my world is interdependent upon his world. When he comes home angry, we all tiptoe around the house so as not to make him angrier. Yet does it really matter what we do? He will feel how he will feel regardless, yet I am still afraid. How then do I become detached?

How do I detach myself enough to work and heal myself? How do I not feel angry when he doesn't come home all night? How do I not resent doing all the work with the children, parents, house, dog, job, bills, school, everything? What do I need him for? How do I stop focusing on his disease and just live my life according to my own beliefs? It feels as though a marriage should take two people to commit to creating the wholeness in the home.

Even though he hasn't drunk for a few months, he is really

miserable. He is angry all of the time. He hasn't changed. He hasn't committed to the program. He simply has through sheer will abstained from drinking. He is a dry drunk.

August 28, 1992

I have an addiction to this relationship and the turmoil that it exudes. I grew up with turmoil, and now my life is full of turmoil. Yet my spirit so desires peace. Am I willing to let go of bad habits, of verbal abuse, of the dysfunctional dialogue? Somehow it is feeding something in me. That is what I must discover, that is the work I must do, that is what I must let go of. I sense many of my painful childhood fears coming to the surface. I am considering divorce. I seek to change my reality. I cannot change him, but I can change myself. Self, get that through your head!

My father died at sixty of alcoholism. I never saw my father drunk. He held a good job, he was a responsible citizen, yet his family life was neglectful, abusive, and cruel. He shattered my mother, he abused my brothers, and he neglected my sister and me. We were abandoned emotionally. He seemed angry most of the time. He was a fireball ready to explode, and my mother always set him off. She tried to keep it all together, like me. She would feed the kids before he got home. She tried to have everything done. She would try to keep peace in the family. She tried to protect us. It didn't matter what she did. He would be angry regardless. We weren't protected.

August 30, 1992

He drank again, and this time he was gone for two days. He never called. I saw his car at the bar at eight in the morning. When he finally came home around three, the kids were gone. We were out in the garage. I fell to my knees; I begged him in tears. "Please get some help. Please let's work together. Let's try to get some help. If you had cancer we would get medication. You have a disease. Let's get some help. Our family is falling apart. I beg you for our marriage, for the children, for yourself. Remember our counselor, Betty. Please, I am bleeding under this pressure. Please, I don't like who I have become. I hate my dialogue with you. I am in pain; you are in pain. Let's get some help."

He pushed me against the back fence. My arms and my back were black and blue. Things are getting out of control, yet how much pain and suffering can I endure? Why is he so angry? God help us. He hates me.

September 1, 1992

This summer I graduated from college with my teaching credential! I have always dreamed of being a teacher, and for some reason, I never lost sight of my dream. Many times I felt like quitting school. I had great reasons to, but I was guided by God to finish. I feel incredibly scared, but I also feel self-assured. I have a great passion for teaching. I feel inspired. I feel as if teaching is something that I am meant to do. I have been blessed with tenacity.

Today is a great, miraculous day. I was incredibly blessed with a job teaching eighth-grade language arts. I cannot believe how wonderful I feel. The principal who hired me said he believed in me, and I had such a great record as a substitute teacher. Even the teachers for whom I substituted asked for me to work there. He also said he was excited by my enthusiasm and effervescence. (I think I need to look up that word.) I hope that I can share my understanding, my passion for life, and my joy for learning with the students. Thank you, thank you, thank you, God!

October 17, 1992

The poetry is within me. Hello, alas, sweet doom. You have returned. My mind has had a break, knowing always that you were around the corner waiting for me to fall again. I have been running from you, sweet doom. I have tried to hide my reality. I have focused on the positive. How do I escape? I lie about my reality. I try to make people think I have it together because this is what I so desperately want. So is my reality real or not real? What am I living, a truth or a lie? As much as I try, I cannot escape what is, and eventually I am faced with the cold bitter reality of my life. I am living with an alcoholic. He is verbally and physically abusive to me, and I am just as much to blame. I am a codependent. I am sick too. I stay here. I tolerate it. I participate in the dialogue. I allow myself to be hurt.

He is drunk and has passed out on one of the beds. Here I am looking for serenity and peace, feeling the bitterness and anger of his betrayal. While I sit and stew with resentment and anger, he is sound asleep, oblivious to it all.

I am truly stricken with sadness not just for the loss of our relationship but also for the loss of our friendship, our trust, and our unity. I feel truly alone in this experience. He has abandoned me emotionally, physically, and intimately. Yet I wonder if I ever had any of these things. I feel so alone. With whom can I share these feelings?

October 18, 1992

I have tried to be honest with him. I have tried to talk about the pain we're in, to express myself, my hurt. I realize the difficulty he must be experiencing. We worked hard to build what life we have together. We began our married life with therapy, three years with Betty. Back then we talked about issues, family, alcoholism, drug abuse, verbal abuse, physical abuse, and the dynamics of a dysfunctional relationship.

Betty helped us understand that if Daddy's head is stuck in a bottle, he is emotionally unavailable for the family. Mother is so worried about Daddy that she becomes emotionally unavailable too, or she tries to be the mother and the father. What Mother cannot do, the children compensate for. They take upon them the missing links in the family, and therefore they develop false identities. We as dysfunctional parents are not the only ones paying the prices for our relationship. Our children pay the price as well.

My brothers and sister paid the price for my parents' dysfunctional relationship. My oldest brother was a heroin addict for years. My other brothers have struggled with drugs and criminal activity. All three of my brothers have been in jail. My sister has struggled with abusive relationships over and over again. I feel sad for their pain, but here I am, and my life is a mess.

My hope in therapy was that possibly with him clean and sober, and with me healthy, we could together break the alcoholic pattern and provide a healthy future for our children and us. This is what is making me crazy. He knows the effects of alcoholism. He has been through therapy. How can he consciously make the choice to drink?

I have chosen to talk with him about this now. I have chosen to work with him now and help this family now. I need to change myself now. I cannot lie and pretend to be happy. We have to be honest with each other so we can heal our wounds, trust again, and build a future for these children! Am I beating my head against the wall? Nobody is listening!

He will not talk about it.

October 31, 1992

It is Halloween again. I am reminded of a year ago. The sadness is still the same. We live in a new house, we drive a different car, but the aloneness, the abandonment, and the lack of family unity is the same. Progression in life is important to me. Have I progressed? This diary is a great reminder of where I have been and where I am going. I am not sure where I am going, but I feel a sense of power come over me. I am searching to find some inspiration to change my life. I am glad I have kept this diary so that I am reminded of my own personal struggles and lack of growth. I sound so sick.

November 3, 1992

I was so inspired today when I met a woman who had God, wisdom, literature, compassion, virtue, and love radiating from her. She inspired me to think that all is possible. My dreams and desires of truth and freedom are not just fantasies of a young woman who knows nothing about life. People really do live that way. Oh, it feels so good to know that I can dream and that I am growing. I was so amazed at the beauty of her world, herself, her children, and her husband. We talked of Indonesia, where children are considered to be closest to God. In the morning everyone scurries around because it is believed that if you do a good deed for someone in the morning, you will have good luck in the day. How simply wonderful. What a world we would have if we all took the time to serve one another each day. I am inspired. I feel hope. Thank you.

November 30, 1992

Today I am ready to have God come into my life. I am ready to greet this day with love in my heart, for love is the greatest foundation for success. I have so much love inside of me. I feel powerless.

December 1, 1992

How cruel can a man be? He seems to have no regard for feelings, emotions, or a person's self-respect. I have no self-respect in this house. I have no life. He is so cruel to the children and me. He is ruthless in his words and inhumane in his approach to parenting. He yells at the kids; he yells at me. He spits on us as though we are despicable. I am at a loss for words. I would gladly cut out his heart if only I had a chance, yet what would that solve? I am full of anger and fear. He is a coward. Anyone who beats up and verbally diminishes women and children is a coward.

January 1, 1993

I am alone again. I am struggling to make sense out of what I call my life. I write continuously of freedom. My spirit is searching so desperately for lightness, yet within these walls it is a battle zone. Do I dare compare my life to that of war victims? Is that too presumptuous? I am sorry. I feel as though any moment I may be victimized, abused, yet the neglect of our marriage is just as damaging. I have no trust. He breaks all his promises. I fear a bomb will drop on my head any moment. What happens to a relationship when you don't respect a man? Is all hope gone? How can he live with me? I am driving him away.

January 20, 1993

Only pain comes to those who wait for it. How can I respect a man who spends his afternoon drinking? All day he sits at the bar, yet it seems so pitiful and sad. How lonely he must be. I feel angry because I am working, teaching, creating, living, learning, yet he sits and kills part of himself. When he is done killing part of himself, he comes home and tries to kill part of us.

I feel hopeless about my relationship, my love, my heart, and my marriage. I am feeling a sense of detachment. I see the pain I've been in. I see the anger I've vented. I see the frustration of the situation. I feel like screaming. I realized today that he is on his own destructive path. He will create his own reality and experience the consequences or karma of his own actions. Why do I think that they have to be tied up invariably to my karma and me? He will do what he will do. I wonder if he will die in peace. At least I have a choice.

January 23, 1993

I came home today to an empty house. The rooms are so quiet. I sense that he is away. Is he at the bar? Is he at work? He has not been home for three days. He never called; he never said a word. After a day or two, when he doesn't come home, I always wonder if he is dead! The kids asked for him. I have tried to masquerade the pain and reality of his drinking. I lie to them and cover up his story. I want to protect them from knowing what is going on. I am an enabler. I participate in his alcoholism. I don't want them to be hurt. I want them to have a good childhood and a happy home. I want to give them a life different from the one I grew up in.

My father died of alcoholism when I was seventeen. Our family was dysfunctional. I cannot protect my children, just as my mother could not protect us. Children know when Mother and Father are not healthy. Children sense and know the family secrets.

My brothers and sister have all had to pay a price for the lack of healthy love, commitment, and unity between our mom and dad. Now as hard as I try to prevent it from happening in my life, I am living the same disaster.

Nothing has changed, except that he is a much more obvious alcoholic than my father was. The pain is the same. The neglect is the same. The shame is the same, and the abandonment is the same. I cannot hide the reality of our life from the children anymore. Children can sense the lack of unity between parents. They can sense the tension and the lack of love that resides here. I cannot fool the children. I am only fooling myself.

January 28, 1993

For the last time I have come home to an empty house. Empty by the standards of abandonment. It was three thirty in the morning when he finally strolled in. Again he is drunk and in pain himself. He seems so alone and sad. He writes me these long letters of apologies, and then he drinks again. His life is out of control. I am left with all the responsibilities of the family, his parents, the children, and the home.

I teach all day, come home, feed the family, do homework with the kids, give them baths, read stories, get them to bed, and correct papers until midnight. He is drunk and passed out on the couch. I cannot save him. It is not up to me; it is up to his will and his soul's desire.

I feel trapped because of all of my tremendous responsibilities. I need to leave. How can I leave my home, his parents, the bills, the mortgage, my marriage, and the dog? The children love their home. They have made new friends and are adjusted to a new school. Do I uproot our lives again? Yet how can I stay any longer in this destructive lifestyle? I cannot detach and heal myself while living under the same roof where he is. I am too connected to his reality. I am too victimized by his illness. I need to make a change.

January 29, 1993

Today is our daughter's birthday. He is gone again. I write in my journal to justify the why and how and to try to discover who I am. I am alone. There is a silent fear that resides in the house, and then there is the silence of my mind. The truth gnaws at me constantly. What am I to do? I see his face in my mind, and I feel as if negativism rules the world. *Let go!* I tell myself over and over. God, forgive him, for he knows not what he does. Please, God, love me. Please talk to me. Please forgive me. Please, God, find me.

February 15, 1993

I am leaving him. We have stopped working, and we have regressed. I am dead inside. I feel murdered. The love that once flourished inside me is empty. I feel drained of my vitality, innocence, virtue, and freedom. He has verbally battered my heart, my mind, my spirit, and me. He has dragged his feet, grumbled, and complained about being a husband, a father, and a provider. He grasps at no beauty. He sees no joy. He embraces no freedom, spontaneity, creativity, or love. What is love to him? Ownership? I am not his possession.

He has had a hard life. He has experienced many levels of his own pain. He has had many tough breaks and made many bad decisions. But don't we all have a choice to use the bad and painful experiences of our lives as learning grounds to grow from? Is it inevitable that a painful childhood will destroy us? Should we allow our history to crutch or handicap us, to ruin our lives? We can choose to turn our experiences into good, to heal our wounds, to search for a better tomorrow, and to give back to the world.

February 22, 1993

Bliss, life, freedom, choice, and the power are within me. I am a person back from the dead, back from war. I sit allowing my stomach pains to calm. I am visualizing peace, calm, center, and focus. I am done. I have given all that I have to give. I have tried to make my marriage work. I have tried not to abandon my marriage vows and the promises I made. I have lived with the guilt, the pain, and the agony of his choices. I am free today because I can make my own choices. I must follow my own heart. I am looking for a place to live with my children.

Freedom for me comes when I follow my spirit. My spirit tells me that there is a choice for me to make. I can be happy. I can be healthy. I can experience joy and discover my true potential. I must let go and face my fears. I do not have to carry the burdens of a depressed man. It is not my responsibility to save him. I have children to raise. I have students to teach, and I have myself to nurture.

This house was my dream too. I helped create this reality. I have put into this house my energy, my love, and my time. I love this place, and I feel a sense of safety here. My dream is holding me here. I need to look at the whole picture. Where have I sold out? Did I compromise my values, my integrity, to buy and live in a home and to have the safety and security of this place? I wanted my children to be safe also. Will I turn my head and not face the reality of my marriage, my codependency, my misery, and his alcoholism so that I can have a home for my children and me?

February 27, 1993

It is time for me to leave. A sadness fills my eyes and saddens my soul. I grieve for my marriage, for I am sure that my life with him is over. My marriage is over. What is it that fills my heart with sadness? What is pulling him away from his family and from himself? I wanted to see for myself.

I went to the bar. The stench was musty and rotten. I could barely breathe. The smell of stale cigarettes, alcohol, and sweat filled my nostrils. My stomach started to heave. My eyes fell upon a sight of gloom. I saw men mostly, desperate, lonely, and full of despair. It was so dark, so dreary, and so sad. My spirit was overtaken by the depression of these men wasting away at the bar, drinking, swearing, and complaining about what life and the world had done to them. I felt that it was a place where lost souls dwell. They all seem to feed off each other's stories of misery. Where is the light? Where is God? I saw a desperately lonely man sitting on a barstool at four in the afternoon. I saw him with his head almost on the bar. He could barely look up. He could barely hold his head up. I had to see for myself.

February 28, 1993

I feel so desperately alone. I am afraid of the dark, yet I long for it. I am afraid to leave him, yet I know I must. I told him I was leaving. He threatens my life. He says if I leave he will burn the house down. He says he will torture me forever and that he will be my worst nightmare. My focus is to be independent and strong. I am willfully trying to raise my children with good positive values, with love, and with a sense of safety. I am trying to discover who I am, to become a whole being.

I am trying to penetrate my own psyche to find out where my injuries began. It is so difficult to get in touch with myself amongst the turmoil and dysfunction of our relationship. I must believe in myself, yet at times I hear his voice in my head. I hear the fear, the inadequacy, the battering truth. I hear the critical voice of my childhood, and I feel paralyzed again. I feel that I need healing so that I can have the courage to move forward.

I tell myself to be calm, let go, and allow God to help. I don't really know how to do this. I wonder if I really know God. I think I will simply just talk to him. He must hear my prayers.

I know in my heart I am doing the right thing. I need to get out of this relationship. I need to fight the voice, to fight the doubt and the guilt, and to follow spirit. Spirit has courage, spirit is willing, but my flesh and emotions are weak. I need to fight the temptation of want and neediness. He does not have the ability to make me feel good about my life or myself; he does not feel good about himself and his life. I need to be strong, and I need to have courage.

There are many reasons why I should leave and a million obstacles in the way. I have already stayed too long. I have justified and sold out my own inner spirit, my own sense of truth. I have tried to reason with myself to stay because I made a commitment to my marriage—I need to take care of the house, the children deserve a family, he may stop drinking, he has a good heart, we used to work together, he is just off the track, he will change, he had a difficult life too, he doesn't mean what he says, he is always sorry after he hurts or abandons us, at least now we have enough money for bills and food, and we have a home. What price will I pay for these things? Will I pay the price of sanity?

March 1, 1993

Alcoholism is a disease. It changes hearts from good into evil. It tempers and numbs the soul, thus allowing good people to hurt, abandon, abuse, and destroy the ones they love, but more so themselves. It takes people away from experiencing their true potential. It destroys families. It destroys lives. So how long should I stay? How long should I uphold the commitment to our marriage? How long should I submit myself to the torture that comes along with his drinking? Do I abandon our relationship? He will not get help. He will not change his life.

Help me fill my heart again with love, dear God. Make right out of what is wrong. A home is not a home without love. A home is what we make it, so for the sake of peace stand by me. For the sake of love, dear God, stand by me. For my children, dear God, stand by me. I don't know why, but I know if I will listen and have courage, thou will guide me. I vow today to listen to thy guidance. I will listen to thy wisdom. I want to replenish the faith in God that I had naturally as a young child. I know God has not left me. It is I who has left God. I suddenly feel courage welling up inside me. I dare to say that I can face the day. Father, bless all those whom I love, know, and care for. Bless all those in need.

I went to my cousin's for the weekend. While I was gone, he had a woman spend the night. They came home from the bar together. She stayed all weekend. Betrayal.

March 2, 1993

I told him I was leaving. He threatened me and screamed at me. He said he will steal our child. He will not let me see her. He said he will not give me any money and will kill me first. He said he would burn the house down. He called me a slut and a whore. He will not leave this house, so I will leave. I don't care. I would rather be dead than live one more day in this torture chamber. He started to get violent. He threw me across the room. My back hit the table. The wind was knocked out of me for a minute. I have great pain between my shoulder blades. I felt so angry, like I could kill him if he comes near me again. He left for the bar.

I am desperate to find some dialogue that is normal. I am looking for acceptance. I feel great sadness in my soul. I am looking for some sign that a positive reality does in fact exist. I pray that some sort of independence will finally shine through.

March 3, 1993

He wrote me a letter. It said he was sorry. I have heard sorry a million times. In his letter he admits that it is his fault and that he is sick. He says that he wants to stop drinking. He is sorry for hurting me. He loves the children and me. He wants to be a good dad and a good husband. After I read the letter, I began to feel sorry for him again. He begged me to not abandon him; he begged me to not leave. He said he would never hurt me again.

I took the letter and put it in a box. As I opened the box, I looked and saw that the box was full of letters saying the same thing. For over two years now, I saved every letter. They were all apologies for verbal or physical abuse, for drinking, and for hurting us. They were full of broken promises. I closed the box, picked up the phone, and called on a condo across town.

March 4, 1993

I was told today I got the condo. My mind desperately searches for resignation and peace. I got the condo on my own merits, on my own income, with my own credit. I have no more excuses. Freedom and peace in my hands, not his. He has no power other than the power I choose to give him.

I feared that I would not get out of the house safely. I have convinced myself that it is just a separation to get my head together. I felt like I should keep him as calm as possible until I got out with the children, until I am safe. I feel as if I am out on a limb. If I look down, I know I will fall for sure. Friends from a local church came and helped us move; he helped too.

My silent prayer today is, "God, be with me. God, be with me. My eyes are closed. I cannot see; please see for me."

March 5, 1993

Today I went to a seminar. We talked about healing, positive choices, alcoholism, and sickness. It was a three-day seminar, and it was just what I needed. I was able to find the courage to begin to face the choices I've made, the mistakes I've made, and the roles I've played in this relationship. He is living his own path. He will choose what he will choose and do what he will do. I am not responsible for fixing him, for changing him, and for saving him.

I am responsible for my own life. It is really heard to detach from all the feelings of anger, pain, and betrayal, yet there is great peace of mind in knowing that we cannot control the lives or choices of other people. One healthy parent is better than two very sick ones. I am just as sick as he is. I have chosen to live a fresh new life, to move on, and to heal my children and myself.

"God, I am blind; please help me see. God, I am scared; please help me to believe. God, I am sure that I have a higher purpose on this earth; please help me to discover my divine potential. I must let go and let God help. I surrender."

March 7, 1993

The children and I have moved, and I have filed for divorce, yet I am filled with bitterness, fear, anger, and an overwhelming sadness. My heart is broken, and I weep and weep. I don't think I'll ever stop crying. I feel a great loss. I have to remind myself minute by minute why I am doing this. If I forget for a minute, self-doubt, weakness, and insecurity slip in. I remember the angry looks, the abusive voice; I remember the anger, the fear, the insults, and the pain. I remember my own ugly voice, yelling, begging, and pleading for a different life.

I look back to this diary and remember the pain. It gives me courage for a day. I am afraid to face the pain; at times it feels as though it will consume me. I feel alone. I know that there is no other way but to face the pain bit by bit, day by day. I hope still to someday find peace. For now, I need to sit quietly with myself and just be.

March 12, 1993

Again I sit in anticipation, dreaming, hoping, and wondering. I think about life with him; does it exist? I have to separate myself from the disease, for how powerful are its clutches. The effects of alcoholism are like the ocean, so strong, so overpowering, so alluring. I am nothing but a small grain of sand amongst the great powers of the sea, of the disease. Daily it pounds on my mind, on my spirit, and on my dreams; then it withdraws again only leaving me so confused, lost, disconnected. Then again I am lured in.

Sometimes I look to grasp for some semblance of peace between him and me. I think about our home together, cooking meals, watching movies, trying to discuss and live life together, and, oh, the children. I wonder if I can let go and allow us to be apart. Can I live this fate I've chosen? Can I move on? My spirit is saddened. I miss him sometimes. Why can't I heal these wounds? I feel so alone. Is it fair to say that all of my life I will feel this sadness, loss, and longing, or am I in a transitional state? Does having pain mean we've done the wrong thing? I hurt so deeply that I cannot find any protection within myself to bandage my heart, to protect my spirit, and to soothe my shattered soul.

March 14, 1993

I believe that there is a God out there. I pray to him every night. I ask him for peace and serenity. I ask for faith and guidance. Where am I going? What am I doing? Who am I?

I am dependent upon him, and that is not healthy. His influence is strong, masculine, and dominating. I wonder why I cannot break away from his spell. Maybe it is not a spell; maybe it is an image or mirage that I've created, but it feels real to me. Maybe the image is my marriage, my dreams, and my projected connection to him. Maybe it is the image of my father. Something inside of me so desires his acceptance. I cannot break away, yet I cannot be near him. I know that I can no longer beg, bleed, and cry for our marriage. All of the love, all of the devotion, and all of the energy in the world cannot stop him from his downward spiral to destruction.

March 16, 1993

Today he called and was dead set on shaming me. He scolded me, screamed at me, spit bile at me. I at first felt like a wounded child. It is a test of trust and faith. I said hello to those old feelings of shame and blame. I wanted to go to the movies with a girlfriend. He somehow thinks it is his business what I do. He called me every name in the book. He accuses me of being with another man. He is trying to impose his reality onto me. He is trying to impose his fears onto me. He has no trust; he lives in fear. He has no self-image, and he is not free to live.

He desperately wants to impose these feelings of inadequacy and failure onto me. He has no confidence in himself. It kills him to see me have a life or even a friend. He is a practicing alcoholic. He is married to the bar. I must stay focused. I must let go. I need to create my own reality and my own life separate from him.

I am sometimes in denial; sometimes I don't want to let go. It is as if a part of me is still addicted to the dysfunctional dialogue. I could hang up the phone, yet I hang on. I don't have to listen, yet I do. I am still in denial. I am afraid. I see clearly, yet I am so blind. I need a person to check on me. I need someone to talk to. Be courageous; be courageous.

One of my children's teachers talked with me today. They are both having problems in school. She hugged me and said that I was courageous! She said she would try to be supportive of the children's emotional needs. We are starting a weekly counseling session for them in school.

March 18, 1993

Because of our daughter, I still end up having to deal with him in my life. When he calls to see her, often he gets off the track of her and focuses on me. His goal in life is to destroy me, and I still go back long enough to listen to a dose of hell. I am in denial over the loss of my marriage, my home, and our family. He is so verbally abusive. He makes fun of every aspect of my life. He ridicules my choices, my friends, my clothes, and my values. When I speak to him, I feel completely suppressed. He is so full of anger, resentment, and jealousy. He tries to suppress every ounce of joy and life that is in me.

I have to continuously remind myself that I am alive. I am free. I can feel peace, joy, and solitude. I rejoice in love. I am free, yet why am I still afraid to take the plunge into the world of truth and self-respect? God, help me.

March 24, 1993

He wanted to see our daughter, so I brought her by. As he sat there ignoring us, eating, reading the *Country News*, I realized how pitifully sad his life has become, how powerless he is over my life, and I felt detachment and far from his grasp and control. I am letting go of my dream of a life with him and my dream of making our marriage work for better or for worse. I am not a quitter, and I am not quitting. I have felt so much guilt about staying until the bitter end.

I have spent years begging for a life that he cannot provide at this time. He has created the world that is safe to him. That is the bar, those people associated with the bar, and his honky-tonk music.

He says that he wants me to be happy. I am surprised at that. I know that his heart deep inside is good. I am letting go of the illusion of family unity and the need to change him, to control his life, to live my life according to his thoughts and feelings. I feel grief for the loss of our marriage, but that is okay. Maybe it isn't our marriage but a dream I once had of family unity, two healthy parents raising healthy children, and more than ever love between a man and a woman.

I dream of a man loving me, cherishing me, and honoring my virtue. I dream of a marriage where two people share the same dreams, the same goals, and the same values. I dream of a life with mutual respect, communication, laughter, and integrity. I dream of love.

March 25, 1993

Why am I crying so? What is it that I cry for? What is it that I want out of my life? What is it that I live for? Freedom is so important to me. I have sadness that comes from deep within my soul. I grieve over the loss of this battle and this dream. I guess it is time for me to fall like the leaf. It is a season of sadness. Someday, though, I hope I will grow and live again. Letting go is so painful. I am afraid of what is out there. Where am I going? Who can I trust? I am entering the unknown territory, the uncharted zone, the final frontier. I look to grasp at little lights in my day. I try desperately to find little hopes, little sparkles of dreams, little lights in the darkness.

March 31, 1993

Tonight he was very verbally abusive on the phone. He called screaming and telling me that if I did not come back to him he would find somebody else. He cannot be alone. He is afraid to face the quiet of the house. He said that he has needs that aren't being met. If I did not come back, then he would have to get his needs met with some other body. I decided to imagine the possibility of him with another woman. He has already been with another woman. It is no secret. I miss my house though. It hurts me to think of another woman in my house. He says that I have a little mind, a little intelligence, and a little worthless education. He makes fun of my sexuality, my individuality. I feel as if I am getting stronger and surer of myself. I think he is stupid and a liar.

The stronger I become, the angrier he seems to get. He screams and yells on the phone. He leaves long cussing messages on my machine. He threatens my life daily. I feel terrorized at times, yet I do not care. I am free. It seems at times that he is a cruel and unusual man. I wonder if he realizes how hurtful his words are, how damaging they are to my spirit. He seems to get bold when he is drinking. He continuously tries to offend me.

He is in complete denial about his alcoholism and his abusiveness, yet I play into it also. I am the classic codependent. I have a choice to not listen, to not try to fix him, and to not engage in the dialogue. I've tried to keep my ground and not play these games. I've tried to stick to the business of the children, bills, and house. Yet somehow I always seem to get sucked into these verbally damaging dialogues. He says

I am damaging my family and tearing our family apart and that I am a quitter. He says I hate men.

It is time for me to get help. As I reread and remind myself of the intricate web of codependency and the damaging reality of the disease alcoholism, I may be able to handle this situation better. I need to become strong. I need to fix myself. I need to protect myself against these lethal attacks and remember that it is his stuff, his reality, his choice. It is not about me! It is not about me!

April 1, 1993

Today again he pled guilt. He cried on the phone. He begged for forgiveness. He is so alone without his family. He said that he is ruining my life. He said he should let me go. I feel a bit cheated. I feel like the last few years have been wasted years. I hope that he finds somebody else. That would be painfully freeing for me. He is a burden.

He says I lie constantly, yet he is living a lie. He thinks I'm cheating, yet he is cheating. He thinks I should report to him whenever I go anywhere, yet he lives at the bar. He is gone for days at a time. He misses his appointments and leaves the kids waiting. He calls and says he wants to see his daughter and then never shows up. She waits on the porch for hours with her bags packed for a sleepover with her dad. He never shows up. He abandons her every weekend. She cries a lot. She doesn't understand why he doesn't come when he says he will. I've tried to talk with him about how damaging and hurtful it is to her. I have decided not to tell her he is coming. I see that he is in pain, but sorry doesn't mean much. He hasn't changed; he has gotten worse.

I am getting stronger. I went to the gym and worked out. I feel really good today. My work is going well. I went to visit my sister. I felt good about being away for a day. I focused on my family, the children, and the people I love. I did not think about him and what he was doing. I am trying to develop my own inner sense of self. Sometimes I feel empty, as if I don't really have an identity. I wish I had a friend to talk to. Since I left him, most of my friends don't call. Maybe they don't know what to say. Maybe it is I who doesn't trust. Do I have the courage to let anyone know the true pain I'm in and the true reality of my life? I am good at hiding my feelings.

April 3, 1993

I cannot even begin to express my frustration. He does not relate to me. He does not understand my passion for life and for the protection of my children. He cannot communicate. I wonder if he cares about these children. On some days he seems to soften and feel badly for the turmoil. Tonight he spoke on the phone of alcoholism sincerely for the first time. I think that this is a breakthrough for him because his denial has been so strong (even after going through an alcohol clinic and knowing the true nature of the disease).

This is how powerful the disease is. It grasps hold of you and won't let go. It is difficult as a married partner to sing a song of love, honesty, reality, and joy when you are faced with denial, rage, shame, and humiliation. To be enmeshed in the disease's dysfunctions feels like battling racism, sexism, and ignorance. These are defense mechanisms for a soul in a lot of pain, but that is a difficult thing to understand. I seem to take everything so personally, like a direct attack on who I am as a person. True detachment is viewing the situation void of self and ego. I am trying to see him in his own light separate from our marriage, our relationship, and me. I am trying to see myself and to discover who I am.

April 5, 1993

I am in pain. I cannot deny it, but that doesn't mean I am doing the wrong thing. He came by to see the kids for a few minutes. He started to smell me, to act sexual. I felt so cheap, so used, as if I am nothing but a toy for his pleasure. All I can do is cry. He said he would come over on Saturday night to see them again. He never showed up. He is not trustworthy. Why am I surprised? How many weekends has he not showed up? Our daughter is suffering. She really misses him.

I feel like a magician at times. I magically weave my day with the children, my job, and my persona. I try to weave harmony and peace in this condo for these children. They are confused and suffering. I need to be an available parent. My desire is to get healthy, to love them, to help them through it all. I am in pain. I want to cry all the time. God, help me and help my children. *Francine, let go.* Someday I will look back at this diary and wonder what I ever saw in him. And why was I so trapped? I need to heal my own inner child so that I can be free of this father figure.

April 14, 1993

It is up to me to decide when I no longer choose to experience this pain. I realize that I must do the work on myself to heal myself. He will continue to hurt me until I decide that I no longer want to be hurt or deserve to be hurt. I am a worthy person. Am I ready to let go of the unhealthy dialogue? Am I ready to move forward and let go of this hell? It is I who consents, who participates, who opens the door to this pain. There was something in my soul that needed this pain, yet I feel the need to heal myself so that I can embrace health. I feel the need to look into my own heart and discover why I need this pain. There is no easy answer. Grief work has to be heart work.

April 23, 1993

Detachment is a word that I have focused on strongly, but what is the true meaning of it? Today I went to pick up a child-support check from him. For the first time in weeks, there was not a flinch in my stomach or a pang in my heart. I felt calm. I looked at the house as a distant memory. He was so angry. His smelly drinking buddy was lying on the couch.

I wondered how much I tried to control this man, how much I tried to make him see life my way, how much I tried to get him to become something that he was not. I saw a side to him that was kind and peaceful, yet it also felt so hypocritical because of his anger and abuse. He will use me if I let him. I feel stronger every day.

When I speak with him now, his anger and his words fall upon deaf ears. I don't feel them penetrating me like a knife. I am somehow protected. I guess that is a start. Maybe it is detachment. I feel as though God is helping me. I no longer view myself as dependent upon his reality. I am separate and only responsible for my children and myself.

May 1, 1993

Today he called and asked me if I would wait for him to get better someday. I think it is good that he sees that there is something wrong with his life. I feel as though I have wasted so many years waiting for him to be there for us, to change, to grow, to self-evaluate. He seems so depressed. He goes to the bar at seven thirty in the morning and stays all day and night. Often he brings women home with him to fill the void and emptiness of his life. I could easily get distracted from my mission of peace, detachment, and freedom if I allowed myself to get caught up in trying to fix his problems.

I feel so calm and peaceful. I don't feel a desire to remedy his life. I feel pity for him, but I don't feel responsible. I feel as though I am moving away from the relationship completely. I feel as if I don't really care what he says or does with his life. It is over. I am ready to get a divorce.

May 4, 1993

Yesterday I spoke with a dear old friend of ours. He has been clean and sober for over seven years. Four years ago our friend helped us when he went through a drug and alcohol clinic. He helped us find counseling and an understanding of the pain and reality of alcoholism. His words on the phone fell on my ears like the soothing comfort of a warm spring day. He expressed his concerns for me. He was surprised that with our knowledge of the disease I stayed in the relationship so long as he was actively drinking. I felt the reality of our lives hit me hard.

Yes, alcoholism sunk back into our lives, and we consented. What did I create? When did I sell out? What role did I play in the nightmare of our lives together? How honest have I been with myself? Why did I play the game so long? Being out and away from the situation has allowed my mind to clear up enough to start asking the right questions and to face my own pain.

He drank for three days straight. He called depressed, suicidal, and incoherent. I gave him our friend's number. Maybe he can help him. It is not my task. I must work on myself. I feel the need to heal these wounds, transform this pain, learn from it, and grow. I dug out all my books on alcoholism and codependency. It is time to face the truth and remind myself of the toxic shame associated with the disease.

June 12, 1993

School is out, and summer vacation is here. I have given my heart and soul this year to these students. When I think about it ending, I feel great satisfaction in a job well done, but I also feel a great loss, for it is again time to let go and move on. Because of the intensity of my own pain, school has been a tremendous blessing and healing source. I find that the joy, love, energy, and uncertainty of the middle-school students have brought me tremendous perspective, humor, joy, and understanding. We ventured this year to many places. I was their teacher, but I was also the learner.

I am amazed at the writing and thinking capabilities of the youth today. They have stretched my mind and expanded my soul. One day we were talking about racism, and I asked, "Where does it come from?"

One of the students said, "It comes from fear, Ms. Cardone. When people are afraid because someone is different, they judge them; then they don't have to change their thinking."

I have been moved tremendously by the minds of these children. I am fearful though of the end of the year and the quiet of summer. I am weary of the quiet of my own home and my own mind. I know the work I must do to heal myself. I know the pain involved in self-discovery. I know the loneliness. I am dedicated to my children, to my job, and to my own self-awareness. I hope I can get through the summer.

July 16, 1993

It is the heart of the summer. I am weary and tired. Some days are really good, and other days are really bad. I am trying to find balance with my pain, my emotions, and myself. I feel the desperate need to call him at times and to engage in some dialogue that is normal, yet that has never happened. Because of the intensity of my pain, I think he should know what I am going through. He should feel bad. He should know our suffering.

The kids seem calmer this summer. We take lots of walks, and we go visit family occasionally. We have friends with a pool. We go there sometimes. They have enjoyed having me home. I am sure my calmness adds to theirs. Our daughter is very emotional though. I feel her pain.

When I talk to him, he is oblivious to our suffering. He reminds me that I left. I wanted this. I have torn our family apart. I feel flooded with guilt, pain, and remorse. What am I doing to my family?

I opened my journal today and reminded myself of the pain I have been in. Does it equal this pain? I can only live one day at a time. The hard part seems to be focusing on myself, not him; focusing on my mistakes, not his; focusing on my own personal discovery.

August 3, 1993

I went to the bookstore and got some books on dysfunctional families and on codependency. John Bradshaw is really hard to read. I threw his book out the window three times already. As I read these books, I realize that there is no easy fix. To be in recovery, to heal the inner child, to do the work to trust again, one must take the hard road. The hard road is doing the grief work, the heart work. I have to face my own demons. I have to look at my family dynamics, the pain and neglect of my childhood, and who I have become as a result.

I have to go back to the work I did in therapy. I remember when I first started therapy. My focus was always what he was doing, how he was hurting me, and the pain he was causing the family. My therapist would ask me, "What's going on with you?" I always felt very uncomfortable talking about myself. I didn't know how I felt. I didn't know what was going on with me. My focus had always been to fix those around me so that I didn't have to feel, discover, and take responsibility for my own healing.

September 15, 1993

I feel as if I cannot do this alone. I read an advertisement for group therapy for women going through divorce. I feel guilty leaving the kids to go to a support group because I know they need me. If I don't get healthier, I am not healthy for them. I called the lady in charge; she said it was twenty dollars each visit. I cannot pay that. Something else will come up.

School is back in session. I have reviewed the student evaluations of my class as well as the journal I kept of the previous year. I did this so I could evaluate what worked and build upon it and take out what didn't work. I am focused for the new school year.

October 21, 1993

I made a mistake in calling him today and asking for child support. He immediately began to be verbally abusive. He screamed at me. He said he wouldn't pay any money because I wanted this, not him. He called me every name you could think of. I tried to convince him that it was his fault for my leaving. I tried to go through lists of things he has done to hurt us: how he has abandoned us, how he has left us to survive on our own, how he would not stop drinking, how he won't help us financially. I tried to convince him that he is an alcoholic, he is sick, he is wrong, he sleeps with other women, he lives at the bar, he has no responsibilities, and I'm still doing everything! The anger inside me was explosive. I feel it damaging my own spirit.

Suddenly I heard my own voice, and I realized that I am still focusing on him, on his mistakes, on his sins. I am giving him my power and my energy. I am still not willing to face my own issues. I am enmeshed in the pain and the desperate need to control his feelings. I want him to be responsible, to feel bad, and to be sorry for what he has done.

I need to let go. If I am truly dedicated to changing my life, then I must stop focusing on him; I must focus on my life. How do I let go of the anger, the resentment, and the pain? It feels all-consuming.

Today I am going to exercise, read, eat healthy, and get through the day.

November 1, 1993

I dread the holidays. I don't care about holidays; I feel too lonely and sad. To feel the spirit of Christmas, it helps to have a home, a family, joy, and a tree. I have no money, I have no home (I hate this condo), and I feel no joy. How will we manage? All I want to do is cry one minute, and the next I feel self-assurance, confidence, and strength. I am going to the gym after work today. I am dedicated to simply being in the moment at my job, with the kids, and at home.

November 16, 1993

I have been dedicated to taking care of myself. I have continued my workout program. I am reading endless self-help books. I simply pray to God every day. I eat well, and because I am so exhausted by the end of the day, I sleep hard. The good days come more often, and the bad days occur less and less. I know I am a worthy child of God and I have a purpose. I try to handle the emotions of my being gently as they come up. Writing is a great source of healing. When I write I find I can let go of some of the anger and the pain. I trust my journal, and I trust my prayers.

It is a time and a season for heart work. I know it will not last forever. I know I will survive and I will be okay. I can't change these feelings now, so I must do everything I can to cope and to endure. Tomorrow is a fresh new day; at least I made it through today.

January 1, 1994

I have avoided his phone calls. He leaves long messages on my machine. He continues to try to get me hooked in his dialogue and in his guilt. I will not look to him for validation of my experiences. I know I am suffering. I know I am having a rough time and have healing to do. I sense that he feeds a desire in me to have acceptance and approval from my father. I continuously looked to him for approval and validation, just as I did from my own father. My father never provided his approval or validation of my worthiness and goodness, and neither will he. The desire for validation needs to come from God and myself.

I am dedicated to turning the power over to God. I have searched for an understanding in my own heart of God, and I realize that I have not been taught of him as a child. I feel him though, in the center of my soul. I feel him in my heart. I sense an innate feeling that he represents all that is good in human nature and in me. I have decided to build upon that feeling and trust in the innate movement of my spirit. When I seek to control others, I ask for God's help. When I feel sad and lonely, I ask for God's comfort. When I feel overwhelmed, I ask for God's guidance. I feel a sense of self-empowerment. I am responsible for my children, my life, and my own sense of happiness. I am getting healthier; I am feeling better about myself. I am feeling God's comfort.

February 4, 1994 (one year since I left him)

I have been a year away from my relationship with him. I have spent this year painstakingly suffering, crying, grieving, and focusing on healing my inner self. I have at times simply prayed to God to get me through the day. On other days, I went to the gym, called a friend, wrote to myself, studied, read, and tried to develop the person that I am. I experienced slices of freedom, detachment, forgiveness, and goodwill. I don't want to carry the anger and the burden of anyone else's pain. I will continue to work, to evaluate, to discover myself.

I have chosen not to give my power away. If I allow anyone the power over my spirit, then I choose to inhibit my own journey. As soon as I allow anyone to abuse my spirit, I am flooded with uncertainty. I transform from a woman of substance, confidence, and beauty to a woman of self-doubt.

Over the past year, at times I dwelt on the feelings of betrayal, on the sickness, and on the hurt. Maybe I needed to go through that anger, that rage. Then I asked myself one day, *is this all you desire? Do you want to spend forever dwelling on hate and anger?* I looked at the state of my hardened heart, and it was sad. True detachment lies in the ability to love the sinner, not the sin. It is important to be able to set limits with people that allow us to love them but also to protect and honor our own spirit.

I know that his behavior and choices have nothing to do with me. If he doesn't show up when he says, it is his choice. If he spends his life at the bar, it is his choice. If he is depressed and suicidal, he can get help if he chooses. Even his inability to hear my pain is not a reflection of me. It is his stuff. I am free of guilt, of responsibility for another person's actions; I am free to be myself.

I do pray for help from God. I have grieved over my marriage, but I have hope that some day I will meet my beloved soul mate. The real journey, the real joy, comes from self-actualization, from self-help. I pray that peace will continue to find its way in my heart and that love will find its way into my life.

February 5, 1994

This year I have focused heavily on healing myself and coming to terms with my own dysfunctional behavior. I have worked hard, cried, and been wounded, but I have also felt days of joy. I know that the road to recovery for anyone is hard. Many nights I felt that to face the quiet of my own mind, my own experiences, my own mistakes, would be too much to bear, yet somehow I survived this year. In those deepest moments I felt God. The pain was intense but never unbearable. I would rather face the pain of my mistakes and let go than carry the denial around with me forever.

Over the past year, I felt as if I was in a fallen, weakened state. I was wounded so many times; I allowed the door to be opened to his abuse. At times I let myself down; I felt as if I had not endured. Often I opened the door to abuse out of fear, loneliness, grief, and loss. I allowed myself over the year to be vulnerable and to trust, only to be used, to have that trust broken, and to set myself back on my road to recovery. The good news was each time I fell, it got a little bit easier to pick myself up again.

I realized that there were things I wanted in my life, so I made a list. First I wanted to experience a sense of forgiveness. I didn't want to have hate in my heart for anyone. I wanted to stop the pain and have peace in the center of my spirit. I didn't want to be hurt, traumatized, abused, or shamed, or to do the same to anyone else. I didn't want to live under anxiety, tension, or fear. I didn't want to focus my life on the needs, wants, and moods of others. I didn't want to control others or feel the overwhelming need to control others because my life and my emotions were out of control. I didn't want to neglect myself, and I wanted to be kind and gentle toward my children. I hoped to not be disconnected from my feelings. I wanted to be honest with myself and see the truth.

Through the grace of God, I believed that all of these wishes were possible; they have become an intricate part of who I am as an individual. Alone I was overwhelmed, angry, and critical, but with God I found mercy, forgiveness, love, joy, peace. I have experienced a change of heart.

February 6, 1994

Recovery is a gradual process of acceptance, awareness, and change. Recovery is an intense healing of the soul. As I looked to God, he made it possible for me to look at my own demons. He made it possible for me to feel sorry, to regret, and to change. He made it possible for me to heal the wounds of my inner child. He made it possible for me to find forgiveness. All the anger and resentment I was carrying for the alcoholic was inhibiting my journey. As I shifted my focus from his faults and his mistakes and began to take a look at myself, I felt my heart change. I sincerely in my heart let go of the control, the fear, and the focus on another human being's faults. I detached myself and thus began my own journey toward freedom and self-mastery.

February 7, 1994

Recovery is a lifelong process, never ending, line upon line. I must crawl before I walk, weep before I sing, hurt before I was healed. As I entered this healing state, my thinking changed; my heart changed. I fell many times, and I am sure that I will fall again. But I am amazed at how quickly I can pick myself up; I believe it is self-awareness.

I realized today how much work I've done. I realized that I have survived under unbearable, unthinkable circumstances. I had to have courage, and I feel good about that. Yes, it has been a year since I left "the alcoholic." I needed this year to heal my wounds, to walk in the quiet embrace of God, to grow spiritually, and to challenge myself.

He has not quit drinking. He has called a million times. Many times I just hung up. Sometimes I listened compassionately to his pain and then hung up, but more often I felt a sense of completeness. His reality and world have absolutely nothing to do with mine. I do not feel compelled to rescue or save him. It is truly out of my control. He must help himself. He desperately tried many strategies to get me hooked.

At times he would call and say, "Why don't you call? You don't care. I am alone, depressed, suicidal. I miss my family. Why won't you help me?" I was able to set very clear limits. I would tell him I could see he was in great pain and he knew where AA was. If he wanted help, he knew where to get it. I told him not to call drunk or in the middle of the night, not to come over without calling. I need my privacy, and I need my rest. If he wanted to see our daughter, he had to be clean and sober. If he did not show up when he said he would, I recorded it for the courts, and he would not be allowed to see her at all. I am getting healthier; I am setting clear limits.

February 21, 1994

Yes, life is a mystery. As I continue to do the work, he has decided to become sober. He said his physical body couldn't take it anymore (that is his reasoning anyway). I struggle with the idea that it is great for him to get his life together. I want to support the good in him. He deserves to heal and find peace also. I have worked so hard to get to this point. I struggle with my love and concern for him as a human being and my own personal progress. I pray for him. That is all I can do. I believe the healthier he is as a person, the healthier he can be as a dad to our daughter.

I have to let God take control. I realize how far I've come and my own need to be healthy. I realize that some people can bring out the best in the other person, while some people bring out the worst. Our relationship together became toxic. He may find his true companion someday. We were not equally yoked.

I thought about what my true desires in a relationship are. I want a man to be available for his wife and his children. I don't want to be abandoned. I want to give and receive love, trust, truth, intimacy, respect, and virtue. I no longer feel the need to be fed by abandonment, hurt, betrayal, fear, and abuse. These feelings used to feel normal; now they bounce off me like rubber. I can accept love in my life. I can accept healthy relationships.

March 1, 1994

He asked if he could pick up our daughter. I was waiting for him to come. He never showed up. She cried and cried. He continues to make promises to her and then breaks them. I spoke with him today. I told him I was frustrated, angry, and disappointed. He is hurting our daughter. The anger inside my heart swelled and was almost bigger than me. I waited until I was in control of my thoughts, and then I told him that I have kept a detailed record of his child visitation. I told him that if he does not show up for her one more time, I will go to court and get full custody, and he wouldn't see her until he can prove to the court that he will do what he says. I will not allow her to sit on the front porch waiting for him one more time. I can set limits for myself but more so for my children.

I am afraid that he will have our daughter while he is drunk. I told him that if he comes over and I smell any alcohol or if he has been drinking, I will not let him have her. I have a responsibility to protect her. I cannot control what he does, but I have to do what I can to ensure her safety.

March 21, 1994

I feel great comfort in reflecting upon my relationship with God. God's love is unconditional. I know that God loves me and him too. I am doing all that I can do to be responsible for my own actions, for my own life, and for my choices. I feel great comfort in knowing that once I do all that I can do to help myself, I can surrender myself over to God's will, and he will ease my burdens. I hope and pray that all I do will be pleasing unto God. God has brought me comfort, joy, and peace. We have struggled, my children and I, but we are free. I have great faith in knowing that I am in God's hands, that these children are God's children, and that we are loved. It has been hard for me to trust God, especially because I have trust issues. In the scariest hour, I felt embraced by the light of God. I believe that in facing my own mistakes and asking forgiveness he has made me strong. It isn't easy to face fears and mistakes. It isn't easy to trust in God.

I feel that it is my responsibility to continue to read, write, learn, evaluate, self-reflect, care for myself, and use my experiences toward good. I wish to develop and discover my divine purpose. I am willing to work hard and to grow as an individual so that I can experience the grace of God and better serve mankind.

I feel incredibly blessed to be free of all the burdens I once carried. I feel blessed to be alive. I feel blessed to have beautiful healthy children. I feel blessed to have a heart, a mind, a soul, and a life. I feel blessed to know that our mistakes can be forgiven. The road to change and repentance is hard but uplifting; my salvation was always in my hands. I had to be willing to accept the mercy and forgiveness of God.

December 7, 1994

Alas, I must rejoice, sweet spirit, for I have arrived. I have arrived. Truly God must feel the joy of my spirit. The true desire of my heart was to know God, to be free, and to find joy. I have experienced a mighty change of heart. I feel grace, peace, and love. I am confident in myself, and the world is a beautiful place. I am overwhelmed with gratitude, for I am so blessed. My heart is open to the world. I feel great love for people. I feel ready to explode. I am healed.

I have two beautiful children. I have a wonderful job that I love. I work with beautiful, kind people. I have family. I have friends. I have God. Thank you. I am greeting this day with love in my heart, for love is the greatest foundation for success.

We may not have money for Christmas, but we have so much more than presents. We have freedom, peace, each other, and the grace of our Savior to reflect upon.

December 16, 1994

My divorce is final. I feel a childlike freedom. He has no control over me. He agreed to let the children and I move back into our house. The kids are happier and safer in their own neighborhood. He agreed to pay child support and have a consistent visitation schedule with our daughter. I have a good job, my children, a home, and God. Thank you. What seemed utterly impossible suddenly becomes a reality.

Best of all, I am not full of guilt and shame, for what he says has no meaning to my life. If he chooses to verbally abuse me, I hang up the phone and unplug it. I set the limit that I have the right to be spoken to with dignity and respect or I will not speak to him at all. As I listen to his words, I am completely detached from his reality. Whatever he says has nothing to do with me. The only power he has in my life is the power I choose to give him. I am free.

Little elves dropped off gifts on our doorstep for the children for Christmas, and an angel brought them new backpacks.

January 1, 1995

I went to drop our daughter off for a weekend visit. When I got there, he had been drinking. I quickly turned and told her to get in the car. She began to cry. We were in the house. He owed me money for child support. He was really belligerent. He started to get violent with me. I grabbed the phone to call the police; he grabbed my head and pushed it into the wall. I passed out for a few seconds, and suddenly I felt the warmth of blood trickle down my neck and back. She was really crying. He felt very bad and got a dirty rag to clean my head and the rug. I managed to get to the car and drive away. I got eight stitches in my head that night.

I wrote it in my diary for the courts. He cannot have her if he is drinking. He will go to jail if he ever touches me again.

January 16, 1995

Life is a continuous journey full of growth and transforma-
tion. As we heal our wounds, we grow to new plateaus. As
we grow spiritually, we move beyond the crippling effects
that keep us from discovering our true nature.

I can honestly say that I have realized the pain and anger
of the past. I realize now that holding on to the anger, the
betrayal, and the lies would not benefit my life in any way.
Nor would holding on to the pain help me to grow spiritually,
emotionally, or psychologically. Letting go of the anger and
finding forgiveness has helped me to grow as an individual.

Forgiveness allows me to pray for him as an individual;
it allows my heart to soften enough to feel compassion and
wish him well. I know that he is on his own journey. The
toxic sickness that comes from alcoholism is devastating and
painful for all involved, but think of the pain the alcoholic is
in. Always I must remember that complete detachment from
the experience enabled me to transform myself outside of the
experience, thus allowing true understanding to take place. I
am void of judgment at this time. God knows our hearts.

I have compassion and empathy, but I will not sell out my
children or myself. I have understanding, but I do not incorporate his thinking into mine. I have love, but I am never
vulnerable to his hurt. I am not responsible to carry someone
else's guilt or their choices.

I have chosen life, liberty, freedom, and happiness—yes,
happiness. The power, the mercy, the love of God is within
all of us. It is up to us to ask and then receive. My transfor-
mation into life occurred through the long process of losing
control, surrendering my will over to the will of God, and

allowing the blessings of God to make possible in my life what was impossible for me alone. This is the truth of the miracle of forgiveness.

January 29, 1995

Yesterday I spoke with him on the phone. I felt the integrity of his words. I felt peaceful, amicable. I felt that my heart was soft and open to his pain. We have battled the years over many issues. He is still heavily drinking. In the past he has blamed the world for his reality, his suffering, his life. He has thrown many daggers at my children and me in his desperate attempt to hold on. He has imposed many damaging verbal nightmares into our home. He has hurt us, but mostly he has hurt himself.

I feel that I have remained diligent in prayer for guidance. I have set reasonable boundaries. When he came over drunk, I would call the police. If he ever touched me again, I would have him arrested. If he called and was verbally abusive, I hung up the phone. He does not do any of these things anymore because I simply have chosen not to play. I could have chosen to continue to listen to the hell he projected and allow it to penetrate my conscious mind, but I decided to view it as an interesting perspective, not mine and not how I choose to perceive the world.

He told me on the phone that he always loved me. He said that the pain in his heart would always be there for me. He said that he would never regret the years we had together. He was grateful for the memories, even though they were fading like shadows. He said I was the light of his life. I brought him joy, and he will never forget me. He said that he made many bad choices, that it was his fault, and that he was responsible. He said that the honest truth was that he had no one to blame but himself. I realized that he had humbled himself. I could hear the tears at the other end of the phone. I felt the honesty in his voice, and I realized that it was good.

I told him that I didn't harbor any anger or bad will. I made many mistakes, and I was sorry for any pain that I caused him too. I told him good-bye.

I felt that I had sown good seeds. Through long-suffering and prayer, I was able to move beyond the pain of a toxic relationship and into the light of peace, joy, forgiveness, and love. The future is bright for me, and I am very happy. I grasp each day with love in my heart, for love is the greatest foundation toward success. I experience the love and the freedom of the spirit of God. He blesses our lives continuously.

February 1, 1995

Goals for 1995:

1. Know God
2. Go to the gym three times a week; exercise every day
3. Keep a clean house
4. Be available, patient with the children, not abandon them every time there is a crisis
5. Budget my money; pay my bills responsibly
6. Scripture study daily; apply the principles to my life
7. Continue to serve in church; learn about the Savior
8. Continue to grow, develop, and learn as a teacher
9. Incorporate relevant, student-centered, meaningful curriculum in my classroom
10. Take pride in my work; give my best
11. Discover and pursue my divine potential
12. Fall in love
13. Work on the house and plant flowers
14. Be happy, experience joy, and share the gospel
15. Feel good about who I am; love myself
16. Be accepting of love in my life
17. Attend a recovery group whenever necessary
18. Build a future for my family

Long-term goals:

1. I want to get married to a healthy, loving, hard-working man. I desire that he is intimate, healthy, spiritual, available, trustworthy, family focused, and that he loves me. Wow!

2. I desire to truly be at a place in my life where I can accept love, goodness, and healthy friendships.
3. I want to let go of the past and move toward the future.
4. I want to love someone too.

February 8, 1995

I believe that each and every person on this earth is a child of a just and loving God. We all have a divine purpose. Our responsibility is to pursue the essence of that divine purpose. In discovering our true potential, we are granted the ability to raise the potential of those around us. As we turn our hearts and minds over to a power greater than our own, as we look into our own hearts, as we change through self-reflection and repentance, his spirit will be with us, and we can perform mighty miracles.

I feel this power in my life. I know every day as I teach that I am assisting in God's plan. I know every day as I love my children that I love his children. I know as I love my family that I love his family too. I know as I love and care for myself that I am showing love and care for his daughter.

February 12, 1995

When living in a natural state of existence, it is important to understand that as humans we have weakness—we make mistakes. Many people have the potential to hurt us; we can love people but not always love what they do.

I feel so blessed in my heart. I feel that I have released my will over to the hands of God. I am so grateful for everything in my life. I am grateful for God's love. I know that as I continue to do the work, to change, to love, God will ease my burdens. I feel the peace that comes with that promise. Sometimes I find myself sitting and listening to the peaceful quiet of my mind. When I have a decision to make, I sit quietly. If I feel warmth and comfort, I know it's right. If I feel confused, off balance, and in turmoil, I know it is the wrong thing to do.

Sometimes I feel so much love my heart will burst. I feel so free and full of life. Thank you.

February 18, 1995

My dearest Diary,

What sweetness it is to have such a loyal, magnificent friend as you. I turned to you in trust to empty the contents of my mind, to reveal the burning in my soul, and to share the tender growth of my spirit as I have surrendered myself over to God. I always find the answers I am looking for. I feel as if I have dialed into the light of the world. As I strengthen my bond and my connection to my spirit, which comes from God, I am able to better serve my family, my students, and the world. We can be equipped with the power to perform miracles to create love and to help others find themselves.

My journey this year is to understand forgiveness as well as unconditional love. As we exemplify and integrate the qualities of humility, meekness, long-suffering, forgiveness, and temperance, we will reap the fruits of love, compassion, understanding, joy, and patience. As we lose ourselves, we truly find ourselves because we give up pride and ego, thus allowing the divine potential of spirit to be.

I realize as a parent I don't own my children. I realize as a teacher I don't own my classroom or my students. I am a servant of God. In all things I wish to do God's will. I have a responsibility to read, learn, of God so that my heart can better know God's heart. I am blessed to have these children of God in my home, so I must nurture them, protect them, guide them, and help them to discover their divine potential. As a school teacher, I have a responsibility to nurture, love, and guide the students. It is not for me to judge them, only to provide an opportunity for them to learn and grow.

March 1, 1995

Spiritual growth is a continuous progression of self-reflection, repentance, change, and love. My blessed children are a challenge. They need love, guidance, and clear limits. I can see that the past few years have been very hard on them. They have difficulty trusting. They struggle with their own self-image and feelings of security. Sometimes my son is rebellious and angry, and my daughter throws temper tantrums that are so severe they scare me.

I struggle with the pain that I've caused them, the guilt that they have had to pay a price for my poor choices, and the truth that I am far from perfect. I have to separate my personal feelings of guilt and shame and simply deal with the issue at hand. They are in a sense a product of their environment, yet the reality of it is a constant reminder of the mistakes I made. I am dedicated and devoted to these children. I will do everything in my power to help them in their lives.

I have to remember that I am responsible for the knowledge I have. In my past, I only did what I knew how to do. As I learned and grew, my life changed. I am very hard on myself at times. Forgiveness for ourselves is just as important as forgiveness for someone else. If I beat myself up, I begin to diminish my sense of self, and thus I alter my potential.

I am devoted to my children. I cannot change the past. I cannot take away their pain or their experiences. I have to progress forward, press on, and endure. God will help us I know, for these are God's children too. I have worked with a counselor who talks weekly with the children. I communicate weekly, sometimes daily, with their teachers so that I can follow through as a parent. I have put them in a school down the street from where I teach. When they get out of school, they come to my classroom. They don't have to go to daycare or after school programs. I have committed to leaving work by four. If I have unfinished work, I take it home and tend to it after they are in bed. We do homework, dinner, and stories every night. They seem to be feeling peaceful. Church has been a tremendous support. They have been able to witness many really good families with positive, loving fathers. I hope to provide role models for them different from what they've seen so far.

March 15, 1995

For many years I have struggled with the idea of why me. Why did I have to have an alcoholic father? Why did I have to grow up the way I did? Why did I have to carry these burdens and solve these riddles? I realized today that everything I have been through has been for my own good. I have been graced with the blessing of these experiences. I have been lucky enough to learn from the pain, to listen to my spirit, to find God, and to change my life. I realize that I am a richer, deeper, more complex, and more complete person as a result of these experiences. I thank God for the opportunity to learn these lessons, to apply them to my life, and to teach others.

I have 174 diverse students in my classroom. As I look into their faces, I see curiosity, wisdom, sometimes anger and fear. Yet all of them seem to be searching for a sense of belonging and acceptance. I feel great understanding for many of them. All of my experiences have contributed to my sensitivity, my understanding, and my compassion as a teacher. I know that these kids will suffer. They have their hardships and their pain. My goal and dedication as a teacher is to give them some tools to discover truth and to know themselves.

My life is on a positive forward stream. I work hard every day. I feel completely blessed in every area of my life. I love being a teacher and a parent, and each morning I greet the day with a "yes" attitude. When I do the work and then turn to him, I feel so close to God. I feel grace, peace, and joy. When I try to do it all on my own, I inevitably fail. Through the great mercy, love, and understanding of God, I am able to find peace and strength in my burdens. I am able to tap in to the true potential and purpose of my life. I have the opportunity to accomplish all that God would have me do!

Addendum

Dear Reader,

I am not a therapist. This is merely my story. Everyone has the potential to experience a mighty change of heart. We can strive toward change; we can become what we never thought was possible. We can change our thinking, our hearts, and our way of living. The greatest joy in life comes when we free ourselves of our narcissistic thoughts and the need to control and fix others and incorporate the true values of love, charity, kindness, and service into our lives.

If ever we find ourselves in pain, abused, dysfunctional, angry, and victimized, we must first recognize that the only power another human being has over us is the power we consent to give them. This is so difficult to see, especially when one is enmeshed in a toxic relationship. As we participate in the anger and abuse, we stifle our own creative potential. It is tremendously difficult to be involved in an abusive relationship and turn our focus off the abuser and turn the focus onto taking care of and healing ourselves. The victory is self-actualization!

Alcoholism is devastating and powerful. Many families are ruined because of the disease. In my marriage the answer was complete detachment. I had to remove myself from the situation in order to detach enough to heal my wounds and surrender over the power to God. Detachment is difficult.

Letting go of the control over another person is difficult, but all of these things are possible through the grace of God. If the true desire of our hearts is to live healthy, free, positive, constructive lives, then we must commit to doing the work and healing and changing ourselves.

Keeping this diary has been a great source of inspiration for me because I have been able to look back and see the pain I was in. I was able to listen to my own desire to have freedom and peace. I was able to see the process and entrapment of the dysfunctional relationship and my own critical voice and judgmental attitude toward the alcoholic. I saw the sad state of my heart, the sound of my critical voice, and the desperately important need for me to change my life.

As human beings we have the ability to tolerate and become desensitized to great amounts of pain. Imagine how we suffer and the injuries we tolerate in our own spirits. Our spiritual journey is the most important work we can do on this earth. As we love one another, as we serve one another, as we maintain eternal perspective, as we realize that this earth is a testing ground, we will progress and find peace.

I know I jumped for joy in heaven in this life to accept the challenges given to me, to face the pain of those challenges, and to grow as an individual, but most importantly I have been blessed occasionally to share who I am and what I am about with another, possibly aiding someone in their spiritual journey.

Healthy love begins when we love ourselves first of all. As we love ourselves, we can nurture and love others in a way that enables them to be strong, not weak; to be healthy, not sick; to be independent, not dependent. Love does not mean abuse, neglect, or giving at the cost of self. If we love people in a healthy, clear way, they are empowered to be autonomous, strong, and effective. Love is not codependent, love is not control, love is not sick. Love is free, empowering, independent, and self-motivating.

My prayer is that we can all be blessed with courage, self-awareness, self-empowerment, and most importantly faith in God. I hope this diary helped you to see that you are not alone!

Yours Truly,
Francine Cardone Miller